MW01171309

Musings of the Miracle Man

Bill Hollace was a quiet man, a man who wouldn't give up despite his massive health issues. He met his challenges with a patient faith that impressed me. More than that, it humbled me.

~ Pastor John L. Sullivan,
Zihuatanejo Christian Fellowship, Zihuatanejo, Mexico

Musings of the Miracle Man immortalizes Mr. Bill's charm and wisdom. You will catch a glimpse of the man I was blessed to know, a fellow John Wayne fan, and a man with a strong fighting spirit who loved life and loved his wife.

~ Emma Hill, Deaconess ICU Mobility Technician

Throughout this book, I hear the words of Mr. Bill as he overcomes death to encourage and instruct those of us waiting for our forever uniting. The insights offered shine light on our daily walk and illuminate the path before us. There is great power within this must-read book.

~Keitha Story Stephenson PhD,
BlueSky Wellness, Bridgeport, Texas

God blessed this man with the wisdom of Solomon. Bill lived his life as a genuine born again believer – a very dedicated, faithful, honest, and energetic person with impeccable character. These attributes endowed our brother with remarkable behavior, which made him unique from others, may we learn from his wisdom.

~ Rev. Dr. Paul Dapaah,
Pastor Faith Assembly of God, Kumasi, Ghana

The words of hope and wisdom on these pages are the legacy of a fearless Marine who shamelessly loved his God, his wife & his country. Bill's journey to complete healing is an empowering example of how God uses tragedy to fulfill destiny.

~ Rachel Dolcine, MPA, CPM,
International Speaker, Entrepreneur & Author

Well worth the read! Encouraging, uplifting and comforting, especially if you or your loved one is going through a time of intense pain, heartache or sickness. Bill's intimacy with the Lord grows deeper through both the joys and the struggles. Beautiful!

~ Pastors Dave and Alice Darroch,
Spokane Dream Center

There lies a love-wrapped tenacity in these pages that will serve to guide us all well in the days ahead – a roadmap of sorts leading to the presence of God Himself. Thank you, Mr. Bill, for the gift of you... and for loving Barb so well.

~ Dawn Stephenson,
Author of *Choosing Fierce – The Making of a Front Line Warrior*,
Coach and Mentor to Kingdom Women

If I had to describe my friendship with Bill in a word or two … I couldn't. Known to say, "I'm no saint, Lord," Bill had a vibrant relationship with his Savior. Through his self-proclaimed "tilted halo" you clearly saw Jesus. Whether serving as a U.S. Marine or battling for his life, Bill was a warrior. To capture the "real" Bill, try to read this book with his life-long Boston accent and a good cup of black coffee.

~ Joseph Lachnit, Sr. Executive Director,
Freedom Has A Face

MUSINGS OF THE MIRACLE MAN

Musings

of the Miracle Man

Words of Wisdom Words of Hope

Barbara Hollace

Published by
Hollace House Publishing
Spokane Valley, Washington

Musings of the Miracle Man: Words of Wisdom Words of Hope
Copyright 2020 Barbara J. Hollace

For more information or to contact the author:
Email: barbara@barbarahollace.com
Website: www.barbarahollace.com

THE HOLY BIBLE, NEW INTERNATIONAL VERSION®, NIV®
Copyright © 1973, 1978, 1984, 2011 by Biblica, Inc.® Used by permission. All rights reserved worldwide. New Living Translation, copyright © 1996, 2004, 2015 by Tyndale House Foundation. Used by permission of Tyndale House Publishers, Inc., Carol Stream, Illinois 60188. All rights reserved.

All scripture references are New Living Translation unless noted by * (New International Version).

Book cover design: Christine Dupre
Book design: Russ Davis, Gray Dog Press, www.graydogpress.com
Book editing: Barbara Hollace, www.barbarahollace.com
Photography credit: Jordan Caskey, JC Media LLC

ISBN: 978-1-7345159-6-1

Printed in the United States of America

Dedication

To all those who have walked through the valley of the shadow of death and lived to tell the story

and

for their families who better understand the precious gift of life.

Introduction

They are not dead who live in hearts they leave behind.
In those whom they have blessed they live a life again.
~ Hugh Robert Orr

Storms are guaranteed in this life. If you aren't in a storm right now, one is on the horizon waiting for you.

We can't avoid them but our lives give testimony about how we choose to navigate them.

In December 1993, God brought my husband, Bill, and I together. We have encountered many storms, but the largest, most ferocious storm began in January 2018. It would be a battle for Bill's life covering two states and five hospitals, multiple afflictions, and the addition of a pacemaker, stents, and a new aortic heart valve. Quickly, Bill earned the title – "Miracle Man."

But it wasn't the damage that was done to Bill's body that defined the journey but rather his attitude and the deeper intimacy with God that marked his path and drew the attention of others.

On April 19, 2020, God took Bill home to heaven. We are left with the beautiful legacy of his life – a man who walked with God and showed us all how to face adversity with grace and grit.

Our words have power. This book is filled with Bill's words – witty responses, conversations with God and me, and prayers spoken in difficult circumstances.

Bill would have been 77 years old on August 28, 2020. To honor his memory and keep his wise words alive, I have compiled this book of 77 words of wisdom paired with 77 Bible verses, words of hope.

Just to give you a glimpse, here is one exchange Bill had with God.

Bill: Do I have any parts of me that say "Made in Japan"?

God: No.

Bill: Are you sure about that?

God: Japan couldn't do what I did in your body this time. (God replaced damaged parts with new ones.)

For the first time, you will read Bill's thoughts as he maneuvered this jagged course to his healing.

My hope and prayer is that you will be encouraged by what you read and that God will touch your life and fill you with hope as well.

This is our gift to you – a peek into the private places of our lives where God transformed us from caterpillars to butterflies.

Blessings!

Barbara Hollace

Contents

1.10.2018

The Day Our World Changed Forever...

Early on the morning of January 10, 2018, I woke up and discovered Bill struggling to catch his breath. His mottled skin verified that Bill was in trouble.

Calling 911 to get help along with crying out to God to save Bill's life and restore his breath was my two-prong attack against the enemy that we faced.

The diagnosis was pneumonia and Bill's heart was in afib (atrial fibrillation). That night while in ICU, Bill had a heart attack. Three days later, he came down with Influenza A, and the next morning had a brain bleed that necessitated transfer by the LifeFlight crew to another hospital for brain surgery to remove the pool of blood.

It is miraculous that Bill survived those first five days. This would only be the beginning of our journey. Fifty days in ICU followed as multiple other things went wrong. The fight for his life continued even while he was sedated and the doctors held out little hope for his recovery.

I believed in the impossible. I believed in God. God can do mighty miracles – saving my husband's life was not too hard for God.

Recruiting prayer warriors from around the world to pray for Bill, they asked others to pray as well. My daily posts of our journey on Facebook and the impact of Bill's healing miracles continued to spread.

Many times, it seemed like the end of the road, but God would say, "No. It's not time. Bill's mission on earth isn't completed yet."

Our journey expanded across the state line into Idaho, where Bill was weaned off the ventilator and had his trach tube removed. After hitting a couple of more snags in two more hospitals, Bill finally came home on June 26, 2018.

His path to recovery continued through lots of hard work and wonderful people to help him on the journey. The most important message is this: Don't give up! Bill got up every day, faced the enemy, and determined he would win with God's help. You can do the same!

Vision

Early in Bill's journey, he was at a crossroads between life and death. We were not able to pinpoint the exact date this happened, but we know it was after his transfer to the second hospital.

Bill had a vision that is important to his story. What follows is Bill's best recollection about what happened.

(The narrative that follows is from conversations I had with Bill and pieced this vision together.)

I was in a dark place, a place between life and death. I was in a lot of pain. I struggled between wanting to die and wanting to live. There were moments when I just wanted God to end the pain but I didn't want to give Barbara up. I wasn't going to lose her.

Then I saw an open grave in front of me. As I looked down upon it, I knew it was my grave lying wide open. I was ready to go. Suddenly God was next to me and we began our conversation.

"Is Barbara going to be okay? Is there insurance so she will be okay financially? I won't go unless she is going to be okay. The pain is so great. I just want to go."

As Bill was speaking and looking at the grave, God blocked his path. Gradually, the grave began to close.

"What are You doing? I could barely get in there before and for sure I can't get in there now."

God replied, "It's not your time yet. There is work to do, move forward."

Bill watched as the grave closed completely.

"I'm no saint, Lord."

"All is forgiven, all is forgiven," God replied.

With God's parting words, the vision of the grave disappeared. God brought Bill out of the darkness little by little so "none of my parts would get messed up."

The journey to Bill's healing continued. It's not where we start but how we finish that matters.

Musings

Live life each day.

This is the day the LORD has made.
We will rejoice and be glad in it.
~ Psalm 118:24

Bill: I am not defeated.

God: Keep talking to Me.

(God and Bill are just beginning a new journey together.)

"No weapon forged [formed] against you will prevail [prosper],
and you will refute [silence] every tongue that accuses you.
This is the heritage of the servants of the LORD,
and this is their vindication from me," declares the LORD.
~ Isaiah 54:17*

I have you. I'm in love all the time.

Three things will last forever – faith, hope, and love
– and the greatest of these is love.
~ 1 Corinthians 13:13

Satan took me down,
but just like Jesus came alive in three days,
I will too.

I have told you all this so that you may have peace in me.
Here on earth you will have many trials and sorrows.
But take heart, because I have overcome the world.
~ John 16:33

Bill: Is this all there is? I mean, I love you, but is this all there is?
Barb: No, this isn't the end. It's only a new beginning.
We have many good years ahead of us.

No eye has seen, no ear has heard,
and no mind has imagined
what God has prepared for those who love him.
~ 1 Corinthians 2:9

You can't beat me.
You can join me,
but you can't beat me.

No, despite all these things,
overwhelming victory is ours
through Christ, who loved us.
~ Romans 8:37

I reasoned that even though I was blind, I had Barb.
Not sure the quality of life we would have but I had life.
Thank you, God.
(For the first 6 weeks after Bill's brain bleed, he was "blind" – all
he could see were shadows. Bill would hear my voice and turn
toward me. Then God restored his sight.)

The LORD opens the eyes of the blind.
The LORD lifts up those who are weighed down.
The LORD loves the godly.
~ Psalm 146:8

I love you.
You love me.
God loves both of us.
What else do we need?

The LORD is my shepherd; I have all that I need.

~ Psalm 23:1

I wanna go home.

Hope deferred makes the heart sick,
but a dream fulfilled is a tree of life.
~ Proverbs 13:12

It's like my brain isn't connected to my legs.
(during a physical therapy session)

I am leaving you with a gift – peace of mind and heart.
And the peace I give is a gift
the world cannot give.
So don't be troubled or afraid.
~ John 14:27

Let's do it!

Because the Sovereign LORD helps me,
I will not be disgraced.
Therefore, I have set my face like a stone [flint],
determined to do His will.
And I know that I will not be put to shame.
～ Isaiah 50:7

I beat the staircase twice
– going up and coming down.

24

I will give you every place where you set your foot,
as I promised Moses.
~ Joshua 1:3*

Bill: God, why when I was sick and felt pain in my body
did Barb have to go through the hard times as well.
Isn't that double jeopardy?
God: No. Bill, while you were sleeping
I was doing a work in her as well.
Today, Barbara isn't the woman she used to be.

She is clothed with strength and dignity,
and she laughs without fear of the future.
~ Proverbs 31:25

Barb: What do you want to eat after you get discharged from the hospital?
Bill: A hamburger and French fries.

Take delight in the Lord,
and He will give you your heart's desires.
~ Psalm 37:4

Thank yoooooou!
Thank yoooooou!
Thank yoooooou!

Always be full of joy in the Lord.
I say it again – rejoice!
~ Philippians 4:4

There is more there than meets the eye
and I don't want to meet it.

The Lord is my rock, my fortress, and my savior;
my God is my rock, in whom I find protection.
He is my shield, the power that saves me,
and my place of safety.
I called on the Lord, who is worthy of praise,
and he saved me from my enemies.

~ Psalm 18:2-3

Listen to your body.
It will tell you what it needs.

Yes, there are many parts, but only one body...
In fact, some parts of the body that seem weakest and least
important are actually the most necessary...
If one part suffers, all the parts suffer with it,
and if one part is honored, all the parts are glad.
~ 1 Corinthians 12:20, 22, 26

Barb: When do you want to go to bed?
Bill: About 10 minutes.
Barb: Okay.
Bill: I'll even go peacefully.

In peace I will lie down and sleep,
for you alone, O Lord, will keep me safe.
~ Psalm 4:8

Some days when I have no aches and pains,
I don't remember that I have this (pacemaker)
or that I'm impaired or handicapped.

But the Lord said to Samuel,
"Don't judge by his appearance or height,
for I have rejected him.
The Lord doesn't see things the way you see them.
People judge by outward appearance,
but the Lord looks at the heart."
~ 1 Samuel 16:7

The anxiety and apprehension are gone –
trying to figure out what's ahead,
what might happen.
The burden has lifted.

Do not be anxious about anything,
but in every situation, by prayer and petition, with
thanksgiving, present your requests to God.
And the peace of God, which transcends all understanding, will
guard your hearts and your minds in Christ Jesus.
~ Philippians 4:6-7*

It's time to move forward.

For everything there is a season,
a time for every activity under heaven.
~ Ecclesiastes 3:1

At church on Sunday, Pastor Dave said, "He smiled."
Bill (smiling): I smiled? I never smile.

A cheerful heart is good medicine,
but a broken spirit saps a person's strength.
~ Proverbs 17:22

We are a team.
We are in this together.

But 'God made them male and female' from the beginning of creation. This explains why a man leaves his father and mother and is joined to his wife, and the two are united into one. Since they are no longer two but one, let no one split apart what God has joined together.

~ Mark 10:6

I have the best of both worlds.
She's just as stubborn (persistent) as me.
And she loves me just as much as I love her.

Who can find a virtuous and capable wife?
She is more precious than rubies.
Her husband can trust her,
and she will greatly enrich his life.
She brings him good, not harm, all the days of her life.
~ Proverbs 31:10-12

Lord, thank you for Your blessings on this day.
Thank you for Barbara staying at my side.

Greater love has no one than this:
to lay down one's life for one's friends.
~ John 15:13

I don't want to interfere with genius.

Anyone who listens to my teaching and follows it is wise,
like a person who builds a house on solid rock.
~ Matthew 7:24

Barb: You see the good, bad and the ugly.
Bill: There ain't no ugly!
Remember I see you when you wake up,
but you take the time
to beautify yourself.

Charm is deceptive, and beauty does not last;
but a woman who fears the Lord will be greatly praised.
~ Proverbs 31:30

A new twist of my brain is
when too much information comes in,
I start to feel overwhelmed.
I need to shut down, shut out the world,
and evaluate what's happening before I move on.

And now, dear brothers and sisters, one final thing.
Fix your thoughts on what is true, and honorable,
and right, and pure, and lovely, and admirable.
Think about things that are excellent and worthy of praise.
~ Philippians 4:8

Bill: Were you there when God created me?
Barb: No.
Bill: Maybe God created my brain differently.

You made all the delicate, inner parts of my body and knit me
together in my mother's womb.
Thank you for making me so wonderfully complex!
Your workmanship is marvelous – how well I know it.
~ Psalm 139:13-14

My mind and body are not accepting limitations.
It's time to take as much change as I can take.

This is my command – be strong and courageous!
Do not be afraid or discouraged.
For the Lord your God is with you wherever you go.
~ Joshua 1:9

1+1= 3
You, Me & God

A person standing alone can be attacked and defeated,
but two can stand back-to-back and conquer.
Three are even better,
for a triple-braided cord is not easily broken.
~ Ecclesiastes 4:12

Three times God asked Bill, "Are you ready?"

Bill: Ready for what? I can only walk a little.

God: That's minor. You have doubled your steps in the last week.

Bill: What am I getting ready for – to do what?

God: Just trust Me.

Trust in the Lord with all your heart;
do not depend on your own understanding.
Seek His will in all you do,
and He will show you which path to take.
~ Proverbs 3:5-6

I've turned the corner.
We, as a couple, can do anything.
I'm not to do it alone but we'll share it together.

Two people are better off than one,
for they can help each other succeed.
If one person falls, the other can reach out and help.
But someone who falls alone is in real trouble.
~ Ecclesiastes 4:9-10

See it through someone else's eyes.
Operate from a place of strength –
not from a place of fear!

For God has not given us a spirit of fear and timidity,
but of power, love, and self-discipline [sound mind].
~ 2 Timothy 1:7

We're going to dance –
maybe sooner than you think!

You have turned my mourning into joyful dancing.
You have taken away my clothes of mourning
and clothed me with joy.

~ Psalm 30:11

You and me and God are the most important.
It doesn't matter what anyone else thinks.

What shall we say about such wonderful things as these?
If God is for us, who can ever be against us?
~ Romans 8:31

I don't like these slow times.

I will be glad and rejoice in your unfailing love,
for you have seen my troubles,
and you care about the anguish of my soul.

~ Psalm 31:7

No longer
"Why can't we?"
but
"What's it going to take?"

For I can do everything through Christ,
who gives me strength.
~ Philippians 4:13

We are happy, crazy kids.

We were filled with laughter, and we sang for joy.
And the other nations said,
"What amazing things the Lord has done for them."
~ Psalm 126:2

I'm walking – that's the miracle itself.
I don't need to explain it.

Jesus looked at them intently and said,
"Humanly speaking, it is impossible.
But with God everything is possible."
~ Matthew 19:26

Everything seems brighter.
It's like I just woke up after being asleep for a year.

The Spirit of the Sovereign Lord is upon me,
for the Lord has anointed me
to bring good news to the poor.
He has sent me to comfort the brokenhearted
and to proclaim that captives will be released
and prisoners will be freed.
He has sent me to tell those who mourn
that the time of the Lord's favor has come,
and with it, the day of God's anger against their enemies.
~ Isaiah 61:1-2

This is a deep healing.
There is no resistance on my part
so God is restoring deeply.

I will repay you for the years the locusts have eaten –
the great locust and the young locust,
the other locusts and the locust swarm –
my great army that I sent among you.
You will have plenty to eat, until you are full, and you will praise
the name of the Lord your God,
who has worked wonders [miracles] for you;
never again will my people be shamed.
~ Joel 2:25-26*

I am awake.
I am tired.
I am lonely.

Then Jesus said, "Come to me, all of you who are weary
and carry heavy burdens,
and I will give you rest.
Take my yoke upon you.
Let me teach you,
because I am humble and gentle at heart,
and you will find rest for your souls."
~ Matthew 11:28-29

You don't know what's happening inside of me – you can't know. God and I are going through this together.

And I am convinced that nothing can ever separate us from God's love.
Neither death nor life, neither angels nor demons, neither our fears for today nor our worries about tomorrow —
not even the powers of hell can separate us from God's love.
No power in the sky above or in the earth below —
indeed, nothing in all creation will ever be able to separate us from the love of God that is revealed in Christ Jesus our Lord.
~ Romans 8:38-39

My tolerance is almost gone.
My mind wants to hurry things up and get going.
My body says "no" – so we wait and go more slowly.

Be still, and know that I am God!
I will be honored by every nation.
I will be honored throughout the world.
~ Psalm 46:10

Sometimes I have self-pity.
God is still doing a work in me
and He's not finished yet.
God is telling me to sit down and wait.
He's still working on it.

Be joyful in hope,
patient in affliction,
faithful in prayer.
~ Romans 12:12*

When will the afternoon naps stop?

Be still in the presence of the Lord,
and wait patiently for Him to act.
~ Psalm 37:7

God to Bill: Sleep while you can because the
time is coming when you will be very busy.
The download starts tonight.
The time for sympathy is over – it's time to sweat.

But now, O Jacob, listen to the Lord who created you.
O Israel, the one who formed you says,
"Do not be afraid, for I have ransomed you.
I have called you by name; you are mine.
When you go through deep waters,
I will be with you.
When you go through rivers of difficulty,
you will not drown.
When you walk through the fire of oppression,
you will not be burned up;
the flames will not consume you."
~ Isaiah 43:1-2

Bill about his singing: The Bible says to make a joyful noise –
but my singing is pure agony!

Shout for joy to the Lord [make a joyful noise], all the earth,
burst into jubilant song with music.
~ Psalm 98:4*

When you get older, you appear wiser
because you take longer to answer.
Think before you speak.

If any of you lacks wisdom,
you should ask God,
who gives generously to all without finding fault,
and it will be given to you.

~ James 1:5

I'm in love.
I'm in love.
I'm in love.

Love never gives up, never loses faith,
is always hopeful,
and endures through every circumstance.
~ 1 Corinthians 13:7

Barb: The weather is nothing to write home about.
Bill (responding quietly with his hands cupped
around his mouth): You are home!

For where your treasure is, there your heart will be also.

~ Luke 12:34*

Bill: Do we win?
God: I don't back losers. Yes, you win.

Those the Lord has rescued will return.
They will enter Zion with singing;
everlasting joy will crown their heads.
Gladness and joy will overtake them,
and sorrow and sighing will flee away.
~ Isaiah 51:11*

If it draws me nearer to God, it's worth it.

We can rejoice, too, when we run into problems and trials,
for we know that they help us develop endurance.
And endurance develops strength of character,
and character strengthens our confident hope of salvation.
And this hope will not lead to disappointment.
For we know how dearly God loves us,
because He has given us the Holy Spirit to fill our hearts with
His love.
~ Romans 5:3-5

Let's go out –
as long as you drive.

You will go out in joy and be led forth in peace;
the mountains and hills will burst into song before you,
and all the trees of the field will clap their hands.

~ Isaiah 55:12

Thank you for watching over my lungs and healing them.
Amen.

Let all that I am praise the Lord;
may I never forget the good things
He does for me.
He forgives all my sins and heals all my diseases.
~ Psalm 103:2-3

(In the middle of the night)
Bill: I love you.
Barb: That was unexpected.
Bill: Expected or unexpected, I love you!

Many waters cannot quench love, nor can rivers drown it.
If a man tried to buy love with all his wealth,
his offer would be utterly scorned.
~ Song of Solomon 8:7

I feel more alive!
(Something good happened during the echogram.)

Light in a messenger's eyes brings joy to the heart,
and good news makes for good health.
~ Proverbs 15:30*

Bill: How are things going?
Barb: Good. I'm getting things done.
Bill: Sounds like someone has an engine.
Barb: What?
Bill: Things are moving like the Little Engine that Could!

Whatever your hand finds to do,
do it with all your might.
~ Ecclesiastes 9:10*

I am a non-existent existent –
one robot controlling another who pays the bill.
(Reference is to his pacemaker. It made him feel more like a
machine than human.)

Guard your heart above all else,
for it determines the course of your life.
~ Proverbs 4:23

Bill looked toward heaven and said, "Thank you!"
It had to be God, there was no other explanation.

Give thanks to the Lord, for He is good!
His faithful love endures forever.
~ Psalm 136:1

We need one of those! (Bill pointing to a corporate jet)
You will be very successful one day.
A new car first – then the jet.

"For I know the plans I have for you," declares the Lord,
"plans to prosper you and not to harm you,
plans to give you hope and a future."
~Jeremiah 29:11*

Thank you for the meal.
Protect us. Guide us. Help us.

The Lord is my strength and shield.
I trust Him with all my heart.
He helps me, and my heart is filled with joy.
I burst out in songs of thanksgiving.

~Psalm 28:7

What can I do today?

He has shown you, O mortal, what is good.
And what does the Lord require of you?
To act justly and to love mercy
and to walk humbly with your God.
~Micah 6:8*

I have you.
I need to stop feeling sorry for myself and move on.

Don't be afraid, for I am with you.
Don't be discouraged, for I am your God.
I will strengthen you and help you.
I will hold you up with my victorious right hand.
~ Isaiah 41:10

Thanks for the results of my heart test and for leading Barbara and I to the Promised Land.

Now faith is confidence in what we hope for
and assurance about what we do not see.
~ Hebrews 11:1*

You're lucky, kid. You can cry.

The Lord is close to the brokenhearted;
He rescues those whose spirits are crushed.
~ Psalm 34:18

Dear Father, thank you for the day and for our blessings.
Lord, come and fix this problem in my soul.
Thank you. Amen.

My health may fail, and my spirit may grow weak,
but God remains the strength of my heart;
he is mine forever.
~ Psalm 73:26

You've been on the edge for two weeks
but that battle is over.

The Lord himself will fight for you. Just stay calm.

~Exodus 14:14

Thank you for this day, for Your blessings, for Your guidance. Look forward to being of better service to You.

Don't copy the behavior and customs of this world,
but let God transform you into a new person
by changing the way you think.
Then you will learn to know God's will for you,
which is good and pleasing and perfect.
~ Romans 12:2

When others talked about this journey, it used to bother me.
Then God showed me it was something
that happened to me when I wasn't aware of it.

The faithful love of the Lord never ends!
His mercies never cease.
Great is his faithfulness;
his mercies begin afresh each morning.
~ Lamentations 3:22-23

I was taught that crying is a sign of weakness.
Sometimes you cry on the inside deep down inside
where no one can see it.

And the Holy Spirit helps us in our weakness.
For example, we don't know what God wants us to pray for.
But the Holy Spirit prays for us with groanings
that cannot be expressed in words.
~ Romans 8:26

Thank you for Your protection and blessings.
Guide us through the dilemmas we face
and through the aches and pains,
and the surprises –
no surprises, please.

Those who live in the shelter of the Most High
will find rest in the shadow of the Almighty.
~ Psalm 91:1

Barb: What will you do when you don't have this hernia anymore? That will be a happy day.

Bill (with a twinkle in his eye): It will be for me.

You will show me the way of life,
granting me the joy of Your presence
and the pleasures of living with You forever.
~ Psalm 16:11

Bless us, O Lord, and even though we don't understand what's
going on with the heart,
we trust You to keep an eye on us.
Thank you.
(Changed TAVR surgery date from 1.29.20 to 2.5.20)

And without faith it is impossible to please God,
because anyone who comes to him must
believe that he exists and
that he rewards those who earnestly seek him.
~ Hebrews 11:6*

God: You make a good team.
Bill: But Barb runs so fast, I can't catch her.
God: When I tell her to run, she runs!
(Bill, Barb and God at the beach in Bill's dream.)

Don't you realize that in a race everyone runs, but only one
person gets the prize?
So run to win!
~ 1 Corinthians 9:24

Bill: How about we celebrate another 30 anniversaries?
Barb: Sounds great to me.
How about 32 more that would make it an even 50?
Bill (smiling): Yes.
(Spoken on our 18th anniversary, two days before Bill died.)

May He grant your heart's desires and
make all your plans succeed.
~Psalm 20:4

4.19.20

The Last Chapter

Any good mystery writer leaves you in suspense until the very last chapter. Well, God is the best author and creator that I know, and He had a surprise ending for us.

Bill was recovering from his February heart surgery at home and regaining his strength. He often remarked about how strongly his "new" heart was beating with the new valve. "My heart wants to run but my body's not ready for that yet."

Daily, we saw improvement, better skin tone, and more light in his eyes. Bill was still contending with a rogue hernia that needed to be repaired once he recovered fully from the heart surgery.

And then God intervened in our story in a new way. Early the morning of Sunday, April 19, 2020, I woke up because Bill's breathing didn't sound right. Turning on the light, I discovered something was wrong and called 911.

The ambulance quickly took Bill to the hospital. As a friend drove me there, we prayed that I would be granted entry to be with him during the current COVID-19 pandemic. Some hospitals were denying all guests.

However, the Lord opened the door for me to go in. The bottom line: Bill didn't have a heart attack or a stroke. In fact, they didn't know what was happening.

At 3:54 am that morning, Bill's heart stopped beating for the last time on earth as he walked into heaven.

There was great rejoicing in heaven even as I was in shock, finding it difficult to grasp that Bill was gone.

There was no pain. There was no suffering in those final hours. The Lord was gracious because He loved Bill so much.

From time to time, I hear Bill's laughter echoing down from heaven. His presence is always with me and God's hand of protection surrounds me.

Today, I give God all the honor and glory because He has done great things for us, He has done great things.

Bible Verse Resource List

Old Testament

Exodus 14:14	139	Psalm 103:2	113
Joshua 1:3	25	Psalm 103:3	113
Joshua 1:9	61	Psalm 118:24	3
1 Samuel 16:7	39	Psalm 126:2	79
Psalm 4:8	37	Psalm 136:1	123
Psalm 16:11	149	Psalm 139:13-14	59
Psalm 18:2-3	33	Psalm 146:8	15
Psalm 20:4	155	Proverbs 3:5-6	65
Psalm 23:1	17	Proverbs 4:23	121
Psalm 28:7	127	Proverbs 13:12	19
Psalm 30:11	71	Proverbs 15:30	117
Psalm 31:7	75	Proverbs 17:22	45
Psalm 34:18	135	Proverbs 31:10-12	49
Psalm 37:4	29	Proverbs 31:25	27
Psalm 37:7	95	Proverbs 31:30	55
Psalm 46:10	91	Ecclesiastes 3:1	43
Psalm 73:26	137	Ecclesiastes 4:9-10	67
Psalm 91:1	147	Ecclesiastes 4:12	63
Psalm 98:4	99	Ecclesiastes 9:10	119

New Testament

Acknowledgements

First of all, thank you to all who prayed us through Bill's journey and offered words of encouragement.

To our family and church family, and friends, we couldn't have done this without you.

Joe and Kelly Lachnit, thank you for walking through the tough places and holding up our arms.

Christine Dupre, Bill's favorite New England Patriots fan, you are a book cover designer extraordinaire.

Pastors Dave and Alice Darroch, thank you for your prayers and for standing and believing for the miracles we saw God do countless times.

Andrea Utrera, thank you for answering the phone that morning when it shouldn't have rang, so you could be with me in Bill's final hours.

Keitha Story Stephenson, thank you for your editing eye and wit and wisdom on this journey.

God deserves all the glory, not only for this book, but for the precious gift of life.

The Man Behind the Words

William "Bill" F. Hollace Jr.

Born in Malden, Massachusetts on a hot summer day, August 28, 1943, Bill remained an East Coast boy at heart until his final breath. A New England Patriots fan transplanted in the middle of Seattle Seahawks country, Bill was loyal to his New England roots.

Bill proudly served his country as a United States Marine. The expression, "Once a Marine, always a Marine" definitely was true in Bill's life. His ability to know the time without looking at a clock was amazing and "Semper Fi" – Always Faithful – defined how he lived his life.

"Bill could see the good in someone that no one else could see" is a fitting tribute to Bill's ability to encourage and challenge others. Bill and his wife, Barbara, spent almost 12 years serving the homeless and low-income population in Spokane, Washington as homeless shelter and apartment managers. It was a labor of love as they helped those who had fallen through the cracks find new hope and healing.

In the last several years, some major health issues redefined his life. But time and time again, Bill rallied from near death to conquer another medical mountain. Bill was fondly called the "Miracle Man" as God saved Bill's life many times. Bill and Barbara gave others hope as they followed his journey to healing. Their love for each other was a bright light wherever they went. Love never fails!

His contagious laughter, witty sense of humor, and kind heart sometimes were masked by a "tough" exterior as Bill made security his business. Bill was a volunteer with the S.C.O.P.E. (Sheriff Community-Oriented Policing Effort) program in Spokane Valley, Washington. A member of Spokane Dream Center, Bill was often found at the door greeting those who entered and keeping a watchful eye out for trouble, keeping others safe was important to Bill.

"Be safe. Stay out of trouble." was often Bill's final greeting as you left his presence.

About the Author

Barbara Hollace

Barbara Hollace is a Christian woman who loves the Lord. God has called her to be a prayer warrior and a writer. Her greatest joy is to pray for others and see God's miracles happen. Through her own husband's health challenges, Barbara has learned that prayer can move mountains in our lives.

Her love of writing blossomed from an early age when she started creating her own greeting cards for family and friends. In 1985, Barbara self-published her first poetry book, "From Dust to Dust." Since that time Barbara has been published in 20 books as well as numerous newspaper articles. She has written 14 novels and is pursuing publication options.

Professionally, she is an author, editor, writing coach, and speaker. Owner of Hollace Writing Services, Barbara's goal is to "identify the good and magnify it!" This includes helping a person get the story in their heart on the page, editing the story, and pursuing publication options. She recently opened her own publishing company, Hollace House Publishing, and will be expanding its reach in the upcoming years.

Barbara has a Bachelor's degree in Business Administration from Western Washington University and a Juris Doctor degree from Gonzaga University School of Law. She is also the Communications Director for Spokane Dream Center church in Spokane Valley, Washington.

For more information about Barbara and her business, go to www.barbarahollace.com.

Author's Note

As both an editor and an author, I understand the joy of holding the finished book in your hands. This book means the most to me of anything I have ever written.

I am so blessed to be able to share the words, the love, the power, and the peace that God blessed Bill with on this journey to his healing.

In God's mercy and grace, I was able to stay at Bill's side through every twist and turn and to fight for his life, both on earth and at heaven's gates.

What I learned about life cannot be contained in just one book; many more books are in the planning stages.

However, as this book is birthed, I didn't expect to be entering my own journey to healing. Just as God was faithful to Bill, so He will be faithful to me.

"This happened so that the power of God could be seen in him (me)." (John 9:3NIV) #Godisfaithful

~ Barb

Other Books

About Bill's Healing Journey

Yes, God! Volume 1
Our Walk of Faith: The Journey to Bill's Healing
Available on Amazon

Coming Christmas 2020
God's Grace on the Winding Road:
The Journey to Bill's Healing

Watch for details: www.barbarahollace.com

Made in United States
Troutdale, OR
11/19/2023